SPYING, SURVEILLANCE, AND
PRIVACY IN THE 21st CENTURY

Surveillance and Your Right to Privacy

Cathleen Small

Cavendish
Square

New York

Published in 2018 by Cavendish Square Publishing, LLC
243 5th Avenue, Suite 136, New York, NY 10016

OCT 2 4 2017   First Edition

Website: cavendishsq.com

This publication represents the opinions and views of the author based on his or her personal
experience, knowledge, and research. The information in this book serves as a general guide
only. The author and publisher have used their best efforts in preparing this book and
disclaim liability rising directly or indirectly from the use and application of this book.

CPSIA Compliance Information: Batch #CS17CSQ

All websites were available and accurate when this book was sent to press.

Library of Congress Cataloging-in-Publication Data

Names: Small, Cathleen.
Title: Surveillance and your right to privacy / Cathleen Small.
Description: New York : Cavendish Square, 2018. | Series: Spying,
surveillance, and privacy in the 21st-century | Includes index.
Identifiers: ISBN 9781502626769 (library bound) | ISBN 9781502626714 (ebook)
Subjects: LCSH: Privacy, Right of--Juvenile literature. |
Electronic surveillance--Juvenile literature.
Classification: LCC JC596.S63 2018 | DDC 323.44'820973--dc23

Editorial Director: David McNamara
Editor: Fletcher Doyle
Copy Editor: Nathan Heidelberger
Associate Art Director: Amy Greenan
Designer: Stephanie Flecha
Production Coordinator: Karol Szymczuk
Photo Research: J8 Media

The photographs in this book are used by permission and through the courtesy of:
Cover Bart Sadowski/Getty Images; p. 4 Bettmann/Getty Images; p, 7, PHAS/UIG/Getty
Images; p. 10 Prisma/UIG/Getty Images; p. 13 DEA/G. Dagli Orti/De Agostini/Getty
Images; p. 16 Myron Davis/The LIFE Picture Collection/Getty Images; p. 19 Universal
History Archive/UIG/Getty Images; p. 24 Wally McNamee/Corbis/Getty Images; p. 26
Mark Makela/Getty Images; p. 29 Vasin Lee/Shutterstock.com; p. 31 Stockbyte/Thinkstock.
com; p. 35 Joe Burbank/Getty Images; p. 37 Charles Steiner/Image Works/Image Works/The
LIFE Images Collection/Getty Images; p. 42 Corbis/Getty Images; p. 48 U.S. Customs and
Border Protection/AP Images; p. 50 AF Archive/Alamy Stock Photo; p. 53 Franck Boston/
Shutterstock.com; p. 56 NurPhoto/Corbis/Getty Images; p. 61 Greg Wahl-Stephens/Getty
Images; p. 64 Africa Studio/Shutterstock.com; p. 67 ESB Professional/Shutterstock.com; p. 71
Evikka/Shutterstock.com; p. 74 Patrick T. Fallon/AFP/Getty Images; p. 77 Oleh Slepchenko/
Shutterstock.com; p. 79 Getty Images; p. 84 Bryan Bedder/Getty Images; p. 86 Carl Court/Getty
Images; p. 88 Stephen Brashear/Getty Images.

Printed in the United States of America

Contents

American spy Nathan Hale was executed by the British during the Revolutionary War.

CHAPTER 1

Search for an Edge

Government surveillance is not a new issue—not by any means. In *The Art of War*, a Chinese military treatise dating back to the fifth century BCE, general Sun Tzu stated, "Enlightened rulers and good generals who are able to obtain intelligent agents as spies are certain for great achievements." Indeed, surveillance in the form of spying and intercepted letters and communications has been going on for centuries. Today, surveillance is obviously much more sophisticated than it used to be, involving hacking and breaches of government security. But the act of surveillance itself is not new, and a look into its history is fascinating.

Surveillance in the Ancient World

Ancient Rome was a hotbed of surveillance activity. Politician and general Julius Caesar, for example, had a network of spies that reported to him about plots against him. He was ultimately assassinated by members of the Roman Senate, but there is speculation that his spies may have tipped him off about the planned assassination ahead of time, and Caesar chose to appear at the Senate anyway.

In those days, surveillance often involved intercepted letters, given that letters were the main form of communication. Cicero, another Roman politician and a famed orator, knew that his communications were being surveyed and wrote to a friend, "I cannot find a faithful message-bearer. How few are they who are able to carry a rather weighty letter without reading it."

Surveillance in the Middle Ages

When the Roman Empire fell and the world moved into the Middle Ages, surveillance continued. The Roman Catholic Church was incredibly powerful at this point in history, and its incredibly powerful surveillance strategy supported, among other things, the Inquisition.

The goal of the Inquisition was to weed out Christian **heretics**. It began in France in the twelfth century, but it spread to other countries in Europe as well, notably Spain and Portugal. From there, it spread to European empires in Africa, Asia, and the Americas. Inquisitors surveyed citizens they suspected of heresy and gathered information that they then used to interrogate, torture, and even sometimes execute suspects.

The Inquisition lasted until the 1820s, except in the Papal States, where it ended in the middle of the nineteenth century, and it is thought to be one of the foundations of modern surveillance. Cullen Murphy, editor of *Vanity Fair* and author of *God's Jury: The Inquisition and the Making of the Modern World*, says that the interrogation techniques used by the inquisitors—which at their base are similar to those used by

Intelligence-gathering techniques developed during the Inquisition are still used today.

law enforcement today—relied on methods of surveillance to support suspicions. "The Inquisition didn't, of course, have the tools that we have today for surveillance, but they had pretty good ones and they collected a lot of information." In fact, Murphy argues that the inquisitors pioneered surveillance, censorship, and interrogation, though evidence of surveillance techniques from centuries earlier would dispute that claim.

Murphy acknowledges that surveillance techniques have changed, but at the core, the method remains the same. "All of those things are much more advanced right now by an order of magnitude than they were centuries ago. Nowadays [surveillance] is done almost automatically—every time you hit the keyboard on your computer or every time you walk by a camera on the street." Surveillance is used to support suspicions and, often, interrogation. As Murphy states, "An inquisition—any inquisition—really is a set of disciplinary procedures targeting specific groups, codified in law … enforced by surveillance … backed by institutional power."

Surveillance in the Early Modern Era

When the Middle Ages ended around the close of the fifteenth century, the world moved into the early modern era. In England, Elizabeth I ascended to the throne in 1558, in a time of unrest in the country. England was in the midst of the English Reformation, in which the Church of England broke from the Roman Catholic Church (under the rule of Henry VIII, who wanted his marriage to his first wife, Catherine of Aragon, annulled due to her inability to produce a male heir to the throne, a request denied by Pope Clement VII in 1527), then rejoined the Catholic Church under the reign of Mary I in 1553. When Elizabeth I took the throne, she was titled Supreme Governor of the Church of England and reintroduced Protestantism into the Church of England.

Naturally, all of this back and forth with the Catholic Church created some unrest in England, which was split between Catholics and Protestants. Many Catholics considered Mary, Queen of Scots, the rightful heir to the throne of England, given that Elizabeth I had technically been declared an illegitimate daughter of Henry VIII when Henry VIII's marriage to Anne Boleyn (Elizabeth's mother) was annulled. Given Elizabeth's Protestant ties, it's not surprising that Catholics lobbied to have Mary take the throne. Elizabeth and Mary were first cousins once removed, and when Mary was essentially cast out of Scotland (due to her marrying a man thought to be the murderer of her second husband), she came to live with Elizabeth in England.

But Elizabeth knew that Mary had the support of Catholics and suspected that she had aspirations to claim the throne, so Elizabeth had Francis Walsingham, her principal secretary, survey Mary and keep Elizabeth apprised of any overthrow plots. Indeed, in May 1582, Walsingham intercepted letters from Bernardino de Mendoza, the Spanish ambassador to England, about a plan to invade England and secure the throne for Mary.

Mary was imprisoned, but Walsingham convinced her that while most of her mail was opened and read, she could correspond secretly through letters hidden in a beer keg. Mary believed Walsingham, and he was able to collect evidence that Mary was indeed involved in plots of rebellion (including the infamous Ridolfi Plot), which ultimately led Elizabeth to order her execution.

Queen Elizabeth I ordered the death of Mary, Queen of Scots, based on surveillance done by the queen's secretary, Francis Walsingham.

Walsingham was somewhat popularly known as a spy for Elizabeth I. Not only did he survey the correspondence of Mary, but he was also sort of the **antithesis** to the inquisitors of the Middle Ages. Where the inquisitors had surveyed, interrogated, and executed convicted heretics in the name of the Catholic Church, Walsingham did similarly to certain supporters of the Catholic Church. An avowed Protestant, Walsingham was fearful of any Catholic uprising that might lead to persecution of Protestants. He intercepted written correspondence and used informants to keep him apprised of the activities of Catholic priests and suspected conspirators in England. He also employed both a **cryptographer** and a man who could break and repair seals so that he could read the correspondence he intercepted without the eventual recipient being any the wiser.

Walsingham's tactics were sometimes questionable, such as his method of tricking Mary into believing that her correspondence smuggled through the beer keg was secure. To detractors, this technique reeked of **entrapment**, but Walsingham argued, "God is my witness that as a private person I have done nothing unworthy of an honest man and, as Secretary of State, nothing unbefitted of my duty."

The same ethical question remains with surveillance today. As secretary of state to Elizabeth I, was Walsingham simply doing his job by monitoring Mary's correspondence? And was it stepping beyond the line to lead Mary to believe she had a secure method of communication when, in fact, she did not?

These same questions come up today when considering the surveillance of people suspected of terrorist plots or other dangerous criminal activities. Certainly, we want to try to prevent acts of terror—foreign or domestic—such as the mass shooting that took place at the Inland Regional Center in San Bernardino, California, in December 2015. One of the shooters in that case, Syed Rizwan Farook, had given officials reasons to be a bit suspicious—he had been in touch via telephone and social media with people who were subjects of an FBI terrorism investigation. If the FBI and other agencies had put Farook under heavy surveillance, would they have known of his plans for the mass shooting and been able to prevent it? It's impossible to say, but using surveillance techniques based on the profile of an individual is problematic as well. A former United States Marine and a member of the Muslim faith, small-business owner Abe Mashal found his business suffered and he missed out on important family milestones when he was barred from flying because the FBI had him on a secret "no-fly" list. With the inability to travel, he missed out on business opportunities and family events for years.

Just as it was during the reign of Elizabeth I, so now is it a fine line between surveying citizens for possible threats to government or national security and unfairly persecuting innocent citizens.

Surveillance in the Late Modern Era

The English and the Romans certainly didn't have a monopoly on surveillance. Maximilien Robespierre, a French lawyer and politician during the French Revolution and the **Reign of Terror** (1793-94), along with his political allies, established surveillance committees to identify, survey, and arrest any people thought to be enemies of the state, including former noblemen, foreigners, suspended public officials, and French nationals who had recently traveled abroad. These surveillance

Maximilien Robespierre used surveillance committees to ferret out people believed to be enemies of the state during the French Revolution.

committees, which were particularly active in small towns, reportedly targeted approximately five hundred thousand people in France. Robespierre defended the practices of his revolutionary government, saying, "The revolutionary government owes to the good citizen all the protection of the nation … If the revolutionary government must be more active in its march and more free in his movements than an ordinary government, is it for that less fair and legitimate? No; it is supported by the most holy of all laws: the salvation of the people."

Robespierre led the French National Convention in releasing a statement of six points of public policy, the second of which, the Law of Suspects, was decreed in September 1793 and stated that people deemed suspicious "who, by their conduct or their relationships, either by their words or writings, have been partisans of tyranny or federalism and enemies of freedom" could be considered **treasonous** and prosecuted accordingly.

Surveillance committees weren't restricted to France during the 1700s and 1800s. Throughout Europe, governments established so-called **black chambers**, or *cabinet noirs* (from the French), usually run in conjunction with post offices, to read the mail of people suspected of various offenses. This was generally done in secret, as the government recognized the problems that could arise if the subjects of the surveillance knew their correspondence was being read. At times, the information gleaned from this surveillance was shared. The black chamber in Vienna, Austria, for example, was known to sell the information it gathered to other European government officials. In a way, it's not so different from companies today that gather personal information and then sell it to other companies—except that in the government's case, they were most interested in identifying threats to security, whereas businesses that sell personal information are most interested in making a profit.

When America was establishing itself as a nation separate from England, mail surveillance and censorship was in full force. The British government would monitor and sometimes destroy the mail going between the various colonies in an attempt to prevent them from corresponding about organizing a revolution against England.

Years later, when the United States was embroiled in its Civil War, postal surveillance was heavy in any mail crossing from the North to the South or vice versa. Further, prisoners of war had their mail heavily reviewed and censored—a practice that was later established as lawful in the third treaty of the **Geneva Conventions**.

Surveillance in the Contemporary Era

Black chambers were thought to have disappeared by the early 1900s, but governments still retained the right to open mail they deemed suspicious or that they felt should in some way be censored. This was common practice during World War I, when governments censored letters sent from the battlefront in an attempt to preserve morale—they felt that if the public knew the blunt truth of what was happening in battle, it might negatively affect overall morale.

This is actually a fairly common practice during wartime, especially when the mail is going to or coming from someone in the military. It is not really a hidden practice—the military intelligence personnel who read the incoming and outgoing mail black out or cut out material from the mail

Men like Nathan Howard read others' mail at the Office of Censorship during World War II.

that they consider questionable. Of course, nowadays more correspondence is done electronically than by snail mail, but the reading and censorship of mail during a period of war is still in practice.

In 1919, the United States founded the US Cipher Bureau, a cryptography office and essentially a black chamber, which, among other tasks, surveyed communications from the Japanese and other members of a 1922 naval disarmament conference. In doing so, it was able to provide the United States government with intelligence that helped it head off a naval arms race by brokering several treaties and agreements among the nine nations involved in the conference. However, in 1929, Secretary of State Henry Stimson disbanded the Cipher Bureau because "gentlemen don't read each other's mail."

World War II was a time of heavy surveillance and censorship. The Allies and the Axis nations both censored mail—military and civil. The United States was among the nations that most thoroughly censored mail, employing nearly fifteen thousand people in this endeavor, under the Office of Censorship. Profiling was used to establish blacklists and whitelists—people whose names were on the blacklist had their mail surveyed, while people on the whitelist were exempt. In the United States, the blacklist was called the US Censorship Watch List, and it contained more than sixteen thousand names. However, the Office of Censorship was a temporary office—it was abolished after the war ended.

During its tenure, the Office of Censorship was particularly interested in keeping an eye on any attempts Germany might make to use neutral territories to conceal assets. Thus, censors working in the office were instructed to look for, among other things, "stockpiling in neutral

The Reichstag Fire Decree

It is sometimes inconceivable to people how the Nazi Party came to power in Germany. How did an entire nation fall under the power of a brutal dictator? There are a lot of answers to that question, but one of the key factors was the Reichstag Fire Decree.

The Reichstag is a government building in Germany. It caught fire in 1933, and Adolph Hitler, who was at that time chancellor of Germany, blamed the Communist Party for the fire (although in reality, the cause of the fire was unknown). He used this to rally citizen support for the Nazi Party, playing on their fears that the Communists were staging an uprising. So convincing was Hitler that he managed to get the president of Germany, Paul von Hindenburg, to sign the Reichstag Fire Decree into law. The decree essentially allowed the president to take power over the government to protect public safety. In other words, it gave the president carte blanche if it was suspected that there was, for example, Communist violence. Eventually Hitler was able to turn Germany into a one-party Nazi state, thanks to this decree.

For private citizens, the devil was in the details with the Reichstag Fire Decree. It was a fairly long decree consisting of six articles. Article 1 suspended citizens' civil liberties, including freedom of expression, freedom of the press, and secrecy of mail and phone communications. Further articles of the decree set forth punishments for offenses, and anyone found to be an opponent of the Nazi Party could be imprisoned or, later, executed.

In other words, if you were a citizen who wrote to another person expressing any sort of distaste for the Nazi Party or Nazi officials, or even if you spoke on the phone about such things, the government had the authority to arrest you and punish you as it saw fit. The loss of privacy led to, for some, the loss of their lives.

The Reichstag fire was one of the catalysts that led to the Nazi Party gaining power in Germany in the 1930s.

countries by the enemy[;] travels by Nazis who fled or had been evacuated from formerly German occupied territories[;] activities of people leaving from Germany and German-occupied Europe, or Germans in neutral countries to Western Hemisphere[;] Nazi political agents in neutral countries[,] in Allied-occupied countries, in Prisoner of War Camps[;] Nazi propaganda agents anywhere[;] German holdings in neutral countries[; and] technical, skilled and managerial personnel operating in neutral countries but of German origin and Nazi persuasion."

After World War II, the Office of Censorship was officially disbanded, but mail has continued to be censored in the United States during other periods of war. Of course, censorship existed outside of the United States after World War II ended; in fact, it was particularly heavy during Joseph Stalin's leadership of the Soviet Union, which began before World War II and extended until 1953. Some scholars have adopted a term coined by Marianna Tax Choldin, a noted scholar on censorship in **czarist** and Soviet Russia: omnicensorship. It refers to censorship that was a part of all aspects of Soviet society, and was particularly prevalent under Stalin. As June Pachuta Farris, bibliographer for Slavic, East European, and Eurasian Studies for the Humanities and Social Sciences Collection at the University of Chicago, writes, "If unexpressed thoughts could have been censored, they would have been, and indeed, in the darkest days of the Stalinist purges, it seems as if they sometimes were."

Stalin was determined to rewrite Soviet history to whitewash any atrocities and paint himself as a Soviet hero. Many of his attempts to do so relied on censoring all forms of media: radio, newspaper, books, and later television. But mail censorship was also a method used under Stalin's regime—although not terribly effectively. As historian Filip Slaveski notes in his book *The Soviet Occupation of Germany: Hunger, Mass Violence and the Struggle for Peace, 1945–1947*:

> The Soviets considered mail censorship essential to their capacity to administer Germany and, indeed, the Soviet Union. However, this by no means meant that censorship was conducted efficiently … Mail censorship became a widespread and haphazard practice … Largely unskilled in the art of surveillance, [Soviet officers] simply delegated censorship duties en masse to the local German administration … Workers randomly opened as many letters as they could, searching for information on a variety of topics.

The Soviets' ineffectiveness at postal surveillance is somewhat surprising, given the heavy importance Stalin placed on censorship, but nonetheless it was an area of relative weakness for the notoriously censorship-heavy government.

Fast Fact

Project Minaret operated only from 1967 to 1973, but in those six years, nearly 6,000 foreigners and nearly 1,700 United States citizens and organizations were included on the watch lists.

When the Innocent Become Targets

The goal of government surveillance in programs such as Project Shamrock and Project Minaret was to monitor threats to national security. The problem is, sometimes innocent people were labeled as potential threats. Some of the citizens put on watch lists thanks to Project Shamrock and Project Minaret might surprise you. Boxer Muhammad Ali was one—though he is perhaps less surprising because he converted to Islam and opposed the Vietnam War, which immediately made him suspicious in the eyes of the federal government. In reality, Ali was no threat to national security. He was not a radical Islamist; he was a peaceful man who devoted his post-boxing life to religious and charity work. Still, his association with a religion deemed controversial by the United States government made him the object of suspicion.

Another surprising target was Martin Luther King Jr. Although King promoted peaceful protest and civil disobedience, his fight for black civil rights was enough to gain him a spot on the watch list. Critics of the Vietnam War, such as actress Jane Fonda, also gained spots of the list, and so did journalists such as Tom Wicker and Art Buchwald. Government officials weren't exempt, either—Senators Howard Baker and Frank Church were both targeted as well.

And therein lies the danger of watch lists: they may indeed help the National Security Agency ferret out potential threats to security, but they may also target individuals who aren't any threat to national security.

However, not all entities behind the **Iron Curtain** were ineffective at surveillance. The East German **Stasi** surveyed East German citizens and reported on any suspicious activities for nearly four decades. By the time the Stasi was dissolved in 1990, it had more than ninety-one thousand officers and nearly two hundred thousand informers.

The United States' Office of Censorship may have been disbanded after World War II, with mail surveillance being done sporadically and on a much smaller scale, but the United States certainly had not gotten out of the business of surveying its citizens. Project Shamrock, started in 1945, was a project in which the Armed Forces Security Agency (AFSA) and later the National Security Agency (NSA) monitored all incoming and outgoing telegrams and passed on any suspicious information to the FBI, CIA, Secret Service, Bureau of Narcotics and Dangerous Drugs, and Department of Defense. The project existed for thirty years, until it became the subject of a congressional investigation, in which the chairman of the Senate Intelligence Committee, Senator Frank Church, called it "probably the largest government interception program affecting Americans ever undertaken." Knowing Project Shamrock was likely to get shut down, the director of the NSA at that time, Lew Allen, went ahead and shut the program down in 1975.

Project Shamrock had a sister program, Project Minaret. While the goal of Project Shamrock was to monitor all telegram communications, the goal of Project Minaret was to share with other agencies the names of United States citizens who were deemed potential threats based on their telegram communications. The names of these citizens were used to create watch lists.

Both Project Shamrock and Project Minaret were overseen by the NSA (although Project Shamrock was initially overseen by the AFSA, the NSA's predecessor). When the Senate Intelligence Committee investigated both Project Shamrock and Project Minaret and became concerned that the surveillance was infringing on citizens' civil

Antiwar activists such as Jane Fonda and Tom Hayden were on a watch list in the early 1970s.

rights, Congress ultimately created the Foreign Intelligence Surveillance Act (FISA) in 1978, which created stricter regulations for NSA surveillance. Under FISA, the NSA needed a court order to survey the communications of people who had been in the United States for more than a year. And if communication was between a foreign party and a person in the United States, the NSA had to gain judicial authorization for surveillance within seventy-two hours of surveillance beginning.

Present-Day Implications

FISA has been amended several times since it was enacted in 1978, and in the present day, citizens' rights are subject to some protection from government surveillance. Yet government surveillance does still exist and is still used in numerous forms. Electronic surveillance has become ever more prevalent as technology has improved.

Is that good or bad? That depends on how it's used. Those in favor of allowing government surveillance suggest that it is the only way the government can try to prevent threats to national security and protect the lives of American citizens. Those against it say it's an invasion of privacy that targets more innocent people than it protects against actual threats. In reality, it's a complicated issue with compelling arguments on both sides.

Surveillance cameras captured this image of Edward Archer shooting to death police officer Jesse Hartnett in Philadelphia on January 7, 2016.

CHAPTER 2

Benefits of Surveillance

Although those opposed to government surveillance feel it is an invasion of citizens' privacy and in some cases a violation of their civil rights, there are valid reasons why the government chooses to monitor people's activities and communications. Sometimes it's a matter of national security, and sometimes it's a smaller-scale but similarly troubling issue, such as child pornography. Regardless of the goal of the surveillance, it is rarely simply to spy on people—there is generally a compelling reason why the government has chosen to employ some form of surveillance in a certain situation. Here are some reasons.

Surveillance for Crime Prevention and Public Safety

One major reason why the government uses surveillance tactics is for domestic crime prevention and public safety. One of the most common public surveillance techniques is the use of closed-circuit television (CCTV), which is widely used in some countries, including the United States. In fact, of the estimated 245 million surveillance cameras installed worldwide in 2014, it's estimated that 45 million were located in the United States. The number of surveillance cameras installed in the US topped 60 million in 2016.

Video Surveillance in Public Spaces

CCTV is also known as video surveillance, and it simply refers to the use of video cameras to monitor the activities in a given area. The video signal may be recorded onto some device, or it may be transmitted live to an area where someone monitors it on a screen—or, in many cases, both. It is called "closed circuit" because the footage obtained from the camera is not broadcast over the open air, like a traditional broadcast television signal is. Rather, it is transmitted over a closed channel to a specific destination.

CCTV isn't only used for crime monitoring. It is sometimes used to monitor industrial processes in factories; it can be used to transmit video of a sporting event to various parts of the arena where it's being held, such as the concession stands, so that fans don't miss a moment of the game; and it can even be used to track the license plates of cars going over toll bridges or driving on toll roads, so that a bill for the toll can be sent to the driver. But crime prevention is indeed one of the major uses of CCTV.

One way the government uses CCTV to maintain public safety and prevent crime is by installing camera networks in traditionally high-crime areas. The Washington, DC, Metro system, for example, has six thousand cameras in place, and the New York City subway system has more than four thousand. Mass-transit operations such as the subway and the Metro tend to be places of higher-than-normal criminal activity, so the use of CCTV can help law enforcement identify a

CCTV cameras are often used in public spaces such as parking garages to discourage crime.

The ratio of people to surveillance cameras installed in North America changed from eleven people per camera in 2012 to six people per camera in 2016. It's estimated that the average American citizen is caught on a surveillance camera more than seventy-five times a day.

suspect if a crime is committed in view of a camera. (CCTV, in fact, was part of what helped law enforcement identify the suspects in the 2013 Boston Marathon bombing.) It can also help prevent crime if perpetrators are aware there is a camera on them.

A 2009 analysis of ninety-three studies on CCTV systems (many in London, but also some in New York and other United States cities) ultimately found that the use of video surveillance resulted in a 51 percent decrease in crimes in parking lots, a 23 percent decrease in crimes on public transportation systems, and a mere 7 percent decrease in crimes in other public areas and public housing communities. These CCTV systems are expensive to maintain, so the question becomes whether the decrease in crime is worth the cost to maintain the system. In some cities, clearly the answer leans toward no—for example, about half of the CCTV cameras in the New York City subway system are broken or otherwise not functioning at any given time.

CCTV cameras are used in some schools, though their use is prohibited in areas such as restrooms.

Perhaps not surprisingly, critics argue that CCTV is an invasion of privacy. But it's worth noting that in a *New York Times*/CBS poll from 2013, 78 percent of the 965 respondents supported the use of CCTV for crime prevention.

Video Surveillance in Schools

Video surveillance is also used for public safety in schools. There are no cameras in areas where a student would need privacy, such as a bathroom or a gym locker room, but there are often cameras in hallways, classrooms, cafeterias, and other heavily traveled parts of the school.

These cameras can help school administrators identify perpetrators in acts of bullying, vandalism, and assault. The likelihood of these acts occurring depends on the school, of course—an elementary school is likely to see the occasional act of bullying and perhaps vandalism, but is not as likely to see assault. However, college campuses are notorious for incidents of sexual assault—a report for the Association of American Universities estimates that 23.1 percent of all female undergraduate students at college experience rape or sexual assault through physical force, violence, or incapacitation. Although 80 percent of these victims will not report the incident to law enforcement, according to the Department of Justice's Bureau of Justice Statistics, for the 20 percent who *do* report the crime, surveillance video can help law enforcement apprehend and potentially prosecute the perpetrator.

Video surveillance also allows school administrators to monitor suspicious people who may be on campus. In the United States, school shootings have become all too common. Many schools have now installed metal detectors to prevent people from bringing weapons onto campus, but that's not the case in all schools—and often, there are ways around them, since most schools have multiple access points (and this is particularly true in college campuses, which are typically composed of many buildings in a large area). If an armed person enters school grounds—be it a student or an outside person—CCTV gives the administration a way to track where that person is and hopefully disarm him or her before tragedy occurs.

Another perhaps less known problem in schools is crimes against students by members of the faculty. This topic has not gotten much attention in the public eye, but it is getting more now that video surveillance is becoming more widely used—and now that there's often someone around to catch an incident on smartphone video.

Students with disabilities are a particularly high-risk group for abuse by teachers and other faculty members. A 2009 report by the American Civil Liberties Union (ACLU) titled "Impairing Education: Corporal Punishment of Students with Disabilities in US Public Schools" found that students with disabilities are subject to **corporal punishment** at a disproportionally high rate, with the range of punishments including "hitting children with rulers; pinching or striking very young children; grabbing children with enough force to bruise; throwing children to the floor; and bruising or otherwise injuring children in the course of restraint." The report details, among others, the case of Jonathan, a fifteen-year-old autistic student in Florida who was thrown face-first onto a tile floor, put in a chokehold, tackled by multiple staff members, and then pinned face down on the floor.

Like many students with disabilities, Jonathan had very limited communication skills and was unable to tell anyone what was happening at school. When he came home from school with a deep cut on his nose and bruises on his forehead, his mother obtained surveillance video from the school and saw exactly what had happened: "They had been picking him up, throwing him into the tile floor like a wrestler. They'd … pick him up by all four limbs. You can see where they're dragging him … They're carrying him like a wild animal."

Unfortunately, this is not an isolated incident. The United States Government Accountability Office (GAO) issued a report in 2009 titled "Seclusions and Restraints: Selected Cases of Death and Abuse at Public and Private Schools and Treatment Centers" that detailed hundreds of cases of abuse and even death in United States schools over the course of two decades—with most of the victims being students with disabilities. The GAO report cited cases in which staff held a seven-year-old face down for hours until the child died, and in which five-year-olds suffered broken arms and other injuries after being duct-taped to chairs or bound by bungee cords.

When video surveillance is used in school settings, appalling cases like these are less likely to occur. Part of the reason why these cases happen so often to students with disabilities is that many of these students, like Jonathan, the fifteen-year-old from Florida, have very limited communication skills or may be nonverbal. They simply cannot report when they are abused, and so their abusers can get away with inappropriate behavior. Obviously, when CCTV is in use, there's a record of an abuse that occurs within range of a camera. It's not a perfect solution— certainly, a person could still use corporal punishment or otherwise abuse a student in an area without a camera. But it is a preventative measure that may help cut down on the number of such cases and is being used more often in special education classrooms.

Video Surveillance as Evidence

Another way in which video surveillance can be used as a tool for public safety is when it is used to document potentially criminal events. In recent years in the United States, there have been numerous cases of suspected police brutality and/or

A surveillance camera showed Trayvon Martin at a convenience store shortly before he was fatally shot.

cases in which undue force may have been used against a suspect based on some criterion—often race.

The case of Trayvon Martin is one of the most widely recognized in recent years. Martin was a seventeen-year-old African American student who was fatally shot by George Zimmerman, a member of the neighborhood watch in the community where Martin was temporarily staying while he visited his father's fiancée. Zimmerman claimed Martin assaulted him and that he shot Martin in self-defense as the two struggled for the gun. However, due to inconsistencies in Zimmerman's account of the events of that night and some unexplained details in the case, many people, including Martin's family, feel that Zimmerman provoked Martin and profiled him based on his race and appearance. Martin was actually returning to his father's fiancée's house after a trip to a convenience store, but Zimmerman suspected that he was a criminal casing the neighborhood.

There were potential witnesses to the altercation, but eyewitness testimony is notoriously unreliable. Social psychologist Gary Wells, who was part of the 1999 US Department of Justice panel that created national guidelines on gathering eyewitness testimony, stated, "Eyewitness evidence can be contaminated, lost, destroyed or otherwise made to produce results that can lead to an incorrect reconstruction of the crime." Ultimately, Zimmerman was found not guilty because the prosecution could not produce enough evidence to prove he was guilty of the second-degree murder charge. This led to outrage among those who felt that Zimmerman had profiled and essentially murdered Martin, who was unarmed when he was shot. If surveillance video of the incident had been available, there would have been indisputable proof of the physical acts in the case, but as it

Onlooker George Holliday took camcorder footage of the Los Angeles police beating Rodney King in 1991.

was, there will always be questions as to whether Zimmerman was indeed acting in self-defense or whether he killed Martin without cause.

There have been many other cases with similarly hazy details, in which a member of law enforcement has killed or assaulted a suspect and it's not entirely clear whether there was reason to do so. This is problematic on a number of levels. Obviously, it's problematic for the victim who was assaulted or killed. When there's suspicion that the assault or killing was not justified, it can become a dangerous situation for law enforcement officers as well, and for the general public.

One of the best-known cases of this occurred in 1991, when multiple officers from the Los Angeles Police Department brutally beat African American Rodney King after he led them on a chase. Video footage of the beating was turned over to the police, and the four officers who actively beat King were **indicted** by a grand jury (although seventeen officers who watched the beating and did not step in to help King were *not* indicted). However, when the four officers were tried, they were found not guilty. Riots in protest of the not-guilty verdict broke out, resulting in looting, burning buildings, and even the beating of a white truck driver who had nothing to do with the case.

Similar situations have reoccurred over the years. In 2016, for example, Micah Xavier Johnson, angry over a spate of police shootings of African American men, fired on a group of police officers in Dallas, killing five and injuring nine.

In the Rodney King case, there was video footage of what happened, and the officers were let off with a slap on the wrist anyway. But the hope is that the use of video surveillance in police vehicles and through body cameras worn by police officers will help prevent such cases from happening again because they will provide absolute proof of what happened in a particular incident. Eyewitness testimony can easily be subject to bias and argued, but video evidence is much harder to dispute. If a law enforcement officer is wearing a camera that will capture events on video, in theory it's far less likely that an unwarranted shooting or assault of a suspect will happen—or if it does, it's far more likely that appropriate punishment will be meted out to the officer.

Much like video surveillance in schools, it's not a foolproof system. But it is a help in cases like these. In the 2015 case of African American Sandra Bland, video from a Texas police officer's **dashcam** proved that the officer who pulled over Bland did not follow proper police procedure. While he claimed Bland assaulted him, which led him to arrest her, the dashcam footage, along with that from a bystander's smartphone video, indicated that Bland had argued with the officer but not physically assaulted him, and he used force to remove her from her vehicle and arrest her. Ultimately, the officer was indicted for **perjury** and dismissed from his position as a state trooper. It was little comfort for Bland's family, given that Bland was found hanging in her jail cell three days after her arrest, but at least it was some measure of discipline against an officer acting improperly, according to police procedure. (Bland's death was classified a suicide, but her family disputes the coroner's finding, saying she would never have committed suicide. There was a surveillance camera trained on Bland's jail cell, but it contained no video recording from the time she died.)

Surveillance tactics are widely used for domestic safety and crime prevention, but they are also used on a larger scale, in an attempt to prevent acts of terrorism.

Surveillance to Prevent Acts of Terrorism

Although surveillance is employed by numerous government agencies in some form or another—whether by simply collecting personal information or by using security cameras and facial-recognition software, for example—the Big Daddy of government surveillance is the NSA. According to a *Washington Post*–Pew Research Center poll conducted in 2013 of more than one thousand randomly selected adults in the United States, 62 percent of Americans felt the government should be allowed to use surveillance to monitor terrorist threats, even if that surveillance intrudes on personal privacy. Fifty-six percent of Americans felt the NSA was justified in monitoring the telephone records of Americans when done under secret court orders. And 45 percent of Americans felt that the government should be able to employ additional surveillance tactics if they could potentially prevent terrorist attacks.

Clearly, potential terrorist attacks weigh heavily on the minds of American citizens, which is hardly surprising in a post-9/11 world and in a world in which ISIS (Islamic State of Iraq and Syria) has claimed responsibility, even if indirectly, for a number of domestic terrorist incidents.

Washington Post columnist Marc A. Thiessen addressed critics of the NSA's surveillance techniques in regard to terrorist threats, saying:

> Terrorists don't have armies or navies we can track with satellites. There are only three ways we can get information to prevent terrorist attacks: The first is interrogation … but thanks to Barack Obama, we don't do that anymore. The second is penetration … This is incredibly hard … That leaves signal intelligence—monitoring the enemy's phone calls and Internet communications—as our principal source of intelligence to stop terrorist plots. Now the same critics who demanded Obama end CIA interrogations are outraged that he is using signals intelligence to track the terrorists. Well, without interrogations or signals intelligence, how exactly is he supposed to protect the country?

Alex Nowrasteh, an immigration expert for the Cato Institute in Washington, DC, found that between 1975 and 2015, excluding the 9/11 attacks that killed 2,983 people, foreign-born terrorists killed only 41 people in the United States.

Certainly, fear about terrorist attacks is a reasonable concern. Where they used to be few and far between, they are now all too common.

The terrorist attacks that caused the most casualties in recent years, of course, were carried out by al-Qaeda on 9/11; nearly three thousand people died. After that, there was a period of relative quiet in the United States until 2009, when Abdulhakim Muhammad (formerly known as Carlos Bledsoe), a Tennessee man who converted to the Muslim faith, shot two soldiers outside a military recruitment center in Little Rock, Arkansas. He later claimed that he had ties to al-Qaeda and that his motivation for shooting the soldiers was "to fight those who wage war on Islam and Muslims."

That same year, on Christmas Day, Nigerian extremist Umar Farouk Abdulmutallab tried to detonate a bomb (famously hidden in his underwear) on a Detroit-bound Northwest Airlines flight. He was unsuccessful, but the government was not terribly surprised by his attempt, since his father, an influential banker in Nigeria, had already alerted them that his son was an extremist with ties to al-Qaeda. The deadliest 2009 terrorist attack on US soil took place at Fort Hood, an army base in Killeen, Texas, when former US Army psychiatrist Major Nidal Malik Hasan killed thirteen people in the name of the **Taliban**. There was initially some debate over whether the Fort Hood attack was motivated by terrorism, but in 2011 the Senate Committee on Homeland Security and Governmental Affairs declared it "the deadliest terrorist attack within the United States since September 11, 2001."

The next year, 2010, saw several terrorist plots against the United States. In May, a car bomb was found in Times

Surveillance footage showed Tamerlan (*front*) and Dzhokhar Tsarnaev before they detonated bombs in their backpacks near the Boston Marathon finish line in 2013.

Square in New York City, but it failed to detonate. It was placed by Faisal Shahzad, an American citizen of Pakistani descent who had ties to the Taliban. Nine days later, a pipe bomb was detonated in a mosque where sixty Muslims were praying. Thankfully, there were no injuries reported. And in October, two separate United States–bound cargo planes from Yemen were found to have explosive devices on them. The devices were found before they were detonated.

In April 2013, three people were killed and more than 260 were injured when multiple bombs exploded near the finish line of the Boston Marathon. Brothers Tamerlan and Dzhokar Tsarnaev were suspected in the attack. Tamerlan died in a gunfight with police. Dzhokar was convicted of the bombings and sentenced to death. The brothers were from the Kyrgyzstan region near Russia. They professed to be Islamists who were not connected to any particular terrorist group but who were supporting the fight of radical Islamists.

Much like the Tsarnaev brothers, Syed Rizwan Farook and his wife, Tashfeen Malik, were not directly connected to ISIS or another extremist group, but they were thought to be self-radicalized and acting based on inspiration from radical Islamist groups. The husband-and-wife team killed fourteen people and wounded more than twenty others when they went on a shooting rampage at a service facility for people with special needs in San Bernardino, California, in late 2015.

Earlier in 2015, Kuwait-born US citizen Mohammad Youssef Abdulazeez killed four Marines and a sailor at a Navy Reserve facility in Chattanooga, Tennessee, after opening fire on a military recruiting facility just 7 miles (11 kilometers) away. The director of the FBI, James Comey, later commented that they had concluded that Abdulazeez "was inspired by a foreign terrorist organization's propaganda."

And in 2016, Omar Mateen opened fire in a gay nightclub in Orlando, Florida, leaving himself and forty-nine other people dead, as well as more than fifty people injured. Mateen reportedly called 911 to alert them that his attack was in the name of **ISIL** (Islamic State in Iraq and the Levant, another name for ISIS) before he was killed. Two years before his rampage, Mateen had been investigated by the FBI for his possible connections to terrorist groups.

It would be impossible for the United States government to identify every possible terrorist and monitor his or her activities. However, a number of these domestic terrorists gained information about how to work with explosives and/or carry out terrorist plots by using the internet. Comey, the FBI director, said in 2015 that social media plays a role in recruiting people for extremist groups. Twitter, he said, "works as a way to crowdsource terrorism—to sell murder." Thus, monitoring social media posts—especially things that are public—could, in theory, help prevent terrorist attacks.

Private electronic communications get a bit trickier. Syed Farook and Tashfeen Malik had professed their commitment to **jihad** and **martyrdom** in private online messages years before the attack in San Bernardino. Comey stated that the couple was "consuming poison on the internet," which led to them becoming radicalized and ultimately carrying out their plot. Although private messages are certainly more difficult to track than something like social media posts, it is possible, and if the NSA had been tracking Farook's and Malik's communications, there's a possibility the attack could have been prevented.

The question is: What would've drawn the NSA's or the FBI's attention to Farook and Malik? The answer: profiling. Much like surveillance, profiling is a hotly debated topic.

Some argue that it's unfair and violates the civil rights of American citizens. A Middle Eastern–born American citizen, for example, may be every bit as loyal to the United States as an American-born citizen. (Foreign-born people don't have the market cornered on attacks of terrorism. For example, the Oklahoma City bombing in 1995, one of the deadliest attacks on US soil, was planned and executed by two American-born, Caucasian men, Timothy McVeigh and Terry Nichols.) A citizen of Middle Eastern descent should be allowed to fly on a commercial airplane without having to go through an extensive search just because of his background, critics argue.

But those in favor of profiling argue that it is a way to keep a closer eye on those who may have links to terrorist groups and may be a threat to public safety and national security. After all, many of the terrorist attacks carried out on US soil in recent years have links to extremist groups in the Middle East—so why wouldn't the government keep a closer eye on people from that region, just to be safe? So goes the argument of those in favor of profiling and heavier government surveillance.

In the case of Farook and Malik, Tashfeen Malik's background might have been enough to arouse the suspicions of the government. Farook's parents had immigrated from Pakistan, but Farook himself was born in the United States and was an American citizen. The only thing that might have drawn a red flag from the government was the fact that he was a devout Muslim who had traveled to the Middle East several times. Malik, on the other hand, was born in Pakistan to a politically influential family. She grew up mainly in Saudi Arabia but attended a university in a part of Pakistan known for jihadist activity. She was also a member of an organization in Pakistan known for teaching very conservative

A Plot Possibly Foiled

One of the NSA's biggest arguments for why their work is valid is that they claim it can help stop terrorist plots before they're carried out. The agency's exhibit A is a case in 2009.

The NSA had been monitoring a twenty-four-year-old resident of the United States named Najibullah Zazi, who was born in Afghanistan. Zazi had made trips to Pakistan in 2007 and 2008, ostensibly to visit his wife, but he eventually admitted that he had received weapons and explosives training during his 2008 trip to Pakistan. In a search of Zazi's computer, the FBI found information about how to build bombs. Zazi denied knowing of the information and claimed he may have accidentally downloaded it.

None of this was enough to arrest Zazi, though. It's not illegal to receive weapons training in another country, and there was no substantial proof that Zazi intended to build a bomb. However, it was enough to make the government very, very suspicious. And so, they continued to monitor Zazi, and the NSA tracked communications between Zazi and a Pakistani bombmaker.

Zazi went so far as to rent a car and drive from his home in Colorado to New York City on September 9, 2009, with the intention of detonating bombs on the New York City subway system during rush hour—an event that would have caused mass casualties, given that a reported 5.7 million people use the New York City subway system on any given weekday. Zazi was aware that the US government had him under surveillance, though, and he received a tip that they might be wise to his plot. So, he returned to Colorado without carrying out his plan.

The government, however, had enough evidence by this point to arrest and question Zazi, and he eventually admitted that he had been recruited by al-Qaeda to carry out a suicide bombing with the New York City subway as the target. He pled guilty to providing support to a terrorist organization, conspiring to use weapons of mass destruction, and conspiring to commit murder in a foreign country.

Zazi wasn't the only participant in this failed plot, and he was not the only one arrested in connection with it. However, he was the ringleader of the United States portion of the operation, and the NSA claims that its monitoring of his communications is what led officials to successfully ward off the potentially devastating attack. This claim has been discredited by those who say that Zazi was caught using conventional surveillance methods, and that crucial information came from British intelligence.

Tashfeen Malik and Syed Farook were photographed by a surveillance camera at O'Hare International Airport.

interpretations of Islam, and some sources claim she had ties to a radical Islamist mosque in Pakistan. She and Farook met on the internet, and she was granted a visa to enter the United States to marry Farook. She did undergo extensive background checks, according to United States officials, but her application for a visa raised no red flags. Still, if the United States government had screened her electronic communications with Farook from the year before her entry into the United States, they would have seen the couple's commitment to jihadist principles, and perhaps the attack would have been avoided.

Would that have been a violation of Malik's civil rights? Maybe. Such a violation could have saved fourteen lives, and it can be argued that saving fourteen lives is worth invading the privacy of one person.

Simiarly, Mohammad Abdulazeez's father, a native of Palestine, had been on a terrorist watch list years earlier because he had donated money to an organization thought to have terrorist connections. He was eventually removed from the watch list, but if the government had placed Mohammad Abdulazeez under surveillance because of his family's possible connection to a terrorist group, they would have seen that he was suffering from drug and alcohol addiction as well as mental-health issues, and they would have seen that he had conducted internet searches about martyrdom and had written about wanting to become a martyr in the name of his faith. They would have also found that he downloaded videos from an al-Qaeda recruiter. And perhaps, when he bought a large quantity of ammunition from a Walmart shortly before the attack, it would have raised some red flags that could have prevented the incident.

Government surveillance is certainly a very thorny topic: At what point does surveillance in the name of protecting public safety and preventing terrorist attacks begin to cross the line into violating citizens' civil rights? One fact that cannot be argued is that it is in the best interest of US citizens to prevent as many such attacks as possible. The question is: Should citizens' right to privacy be compromised to do that?

WAR IS PEACE
FREEDOM IS SLAVERY
IGNORANCE I

Big Brother, the subject of George Orwell's *Nineteen Eighty-Four*, watches a crowd in a scene from the film.

CHAPTER 3

Surveillance Overreach

I n George Orwell's acclaimed novel *Nineteen Eighty-Four*, the protagonist, Winston Smith, lives in Oceania, a nation where the ruling party controls every part of people's lives—what they do, what they read, what they write, and even what they think. The party does this in large part by using sophisticated surveillance techniques that allow them to watch and listen to citizens all day, every day. Over it all presides a figure called Big Brother—and so, the people in *Nineteen Eighty-Four* are always aware that Big Brother is watching.

The novel was written in 1949 and was a work of fiction, though certainly there were strong parallels with the surveillance done in Stalin's Soviet Union and in Nazi Germany. Orwell himself brought up Hitler and Stalin when writing to Noel Willmett about the general ideas that would later be central to his novel: "On the whole the English intelligentsia have opposed Hitler, but only at the price of accepting Stalin. Most of them are perfectly ready for dictatorial methods, secret police, systematic falsification of history etc. so long as they feel that it is on 'our' side." Orwell was concerned that a system of **totalitarianism** would take over if the public accepted methods such as surveillance, control of the media, and the use of secret police as being reasonable for the government to use in the name of safety.

Orwell expressed these fears more than seventy years ago, but even now, when people fear **fascist** or totalitarian regimes may be creeping in or they fear that government surveillance is going over the line of what's acceptable, they cite the world in Orwell's *Nineteen Eighty-Four* and remark about the government being like Big Brother.

In *Nineteen Eighty-Four*, Smith's concerns were reasonable—by the end of the book, he has surrendered his individuality (not to mention his love) to the party and is yet another disciple of Big Brother. What started as the party surveying citizens in Oceania ended with the citizens being little more than government-controlled automatons, incapable of (or unwilling to entertain) independent thought.

And so, it makes sense to consider the topic of government surveillance today in a similar manner. Orwell's novel was obviously exaggerated for dramatic effect, but there is a thread of a very real danger running through it—one that still concerns citizens today.

Invasion of Privacy

One of the biggest arguments against government surveillance is the loss of privacy for individuals. Just as Winston Smith's every move was tracked by Big Brother's cameras in *Nineteen Eighty-Four*, opponents of surveillance worry that current surveillance technology could easily become all-encompassing.

Currently, there are individual surveillance systems—often using facial-recognition software—all across the

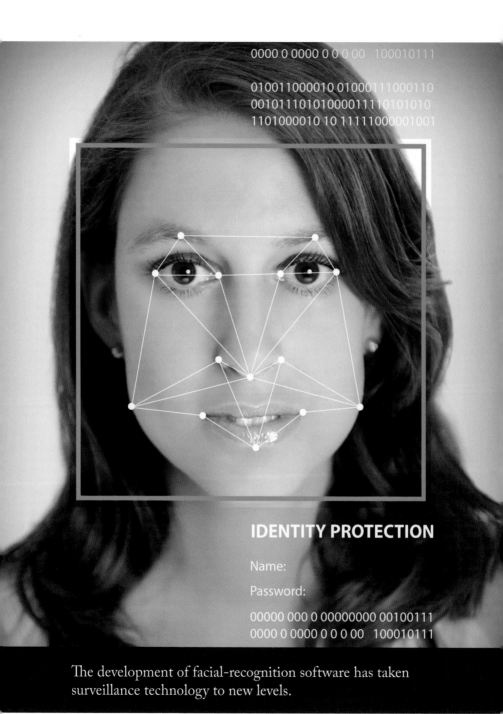

IDENTITY PROTECTION

Name:

Password:

00000 000 0 00000000 00100111
0000 0 0000 0 0 0 00 100010111

The development of facial-recognition software has taken surveillance technology to new levels.

country, but they operate largely separately, maintained by different federal and local authorities. So if a person was a political activist attending political protests in different locations, the government as a whole might not currently be able to easily track his or her movements.

But fast-forward just a bit, to a time when these surveillance systems may be linked. It's not an outlandish idea—a 2016 report by the Government Accountability Office stated that sixteen states had given the FBI access to Department of Motor Vehicles photo records so it could expand its facial-recognition database for surveillance purposes.

Jennifer Lynch, an attorney for an internet civil liberties organization, says, "What concerns me is if all of those cameras get linked together at some point, and if we apply facial recognition on the back end, we'll be able to track people wherever they go." That same person attending political protests in three or four major cities could then easily be tracked.

Sometimes, tracking people might be a *good* thing. If that political protestor is a violent protestor intent on causing harm, then tracking his or her movements might not be a bad idea. However, doing so is a very slippery slope in the eyes of many. If we can track one person's every move through linked surveillance systems, then we can track anyone's every move through linked surveillance systems. And a great many people aren't fond of that idea.

It's human nature to want some privacy in your life. What if you're involved in a relationship that you'd like to keep private? What if you're seeking treatment for a condition that carries with it a stigma or could potentially threaten your job, such as alcoholism or drug addiction? Or what if you're the unfortunate victim of a clever stalker? In all such

From 1992 to 2013, the United States Justice Department and the Drug Enforcement Agency collected data on billions of phone calls to and from 116 countries linked to drug trafficking.

cases, having an official record of your every movement is probably *not* desirable.

And where does it end? Who makes the call about whether it's fair to track the political protestor's every move but *not* the person seeking treatment for alcohol addiction? The government? That leads to another very slippery slope in which we're giving the government a great deal of power over our lives that it may not be wise to grant. With surveillance, it's a bit of an all-or-nothing proposition. If CCTV cameras are present, they're monitoring *everyone*—they don't simply turn on when a suspicious person is in their range. So while many people agree that in a perfect world it would be good for the government to be able to keep an eye on people who are a potential threat to public safety or national security, many people argue that it's just not worth the cost: the loss of privacy for everyone.

PRISM Problem

CCTV and surveillance cameras aren't the only form of surveillance that can be considered an invasion of privacy. One major surveillance tool that has come under fire for

At a demonstration in Germany, a protestor shows his unhappiness with the PRISM program.

invading people's privacy is a program code-named PRISM, an NSA surveillance tool.

There are disagreements about where the name "PRISM" comes from. What is known is that, as of 2013, PRISM collected internet communications data from nine major US service providers, including Microsoft, Yahoo, Google, Facebook, Paltalk, AOL, Skype, YouTube, and Apple—reportedly directly from these providers' servers. The internet communication forms collected were emails, documents, photos, audio and video chats, and internet connection logs.

When the *Washington Post* broke a story in mid-2013 about the use of PRISM and how the FBI and the

NSA were employing it to survey people's internet usage, even high officials at several of the providers were unaware that PRISM had been used for years to survey data from their servers. Steve Dowling from Apple stated, "We have never heard of PRISM. We do not provide any government agency with direct access to our servers, and any government agency requesting customer data must get a court order." Joe Sullivan, Facebook's chief security officer, echoed a similar sentiment: "We do not provide any government organization with direct access to Facebook servers. When Facebook is asked for data or information about specific individuals, we carefully scrutinize any such request for compliance with all applicable laws, and provide information only to the extent required by law."

But that's where it gets sticky. The GCHQ—the British intelligence and security body, essentially the UK equivalent of the NSA—similarly mines data in a program set up by the NSA. Whether or not officials at these service providers were aware of it, this data *could* be mined without a warrant, thanks to loopholes in the law and arrangements made between governments. The Investigatory Powers Tribunal—the body that keeps watch on the UK government's surveillance activities—revealed in late 2014 that British intelligence agencies could freely access data collected through PRISM if it was "not technically feasible" to obtain a warrant and that they could keep the content for up to two years. In response, the deputy director of Privacy International, Eric King, stated in a National Council for Civil Liberties press release, "We now know that data from any call, internet search, or website you visited over the past two years could be stored in GCHQ's database and analyzed at will, all without a warrant to collect it in the first place."

This is not limited to the UK, either. In late 2013, documents leaked by **whistleblower** Edward Snowden revealed that a US loophole allows the NSA to monitor citizens' communications without a warrant. Basically, Section 702 of the FISA Amendments Act allows the NSA to survey, without a warrant, the communications of non-US citizens who are outside of the United States at the point of data collection. Sounds like ordinary American citizens within the US are protected, right? Not quite.

The NSA and other intelligence agencies have acknowledged that the data-collection process on these individuals has some collateral damage: When gathering communications data on these individuals, the NSA databases sometimes inadvertently collect the data on the domestic communications of US citizens. This is a common issue known as incidental collection. And, as it turns out, the NSA has the authority to monitor without a warrant this data that is incidentally collected—even if the NSA has no reason to suspect the persons from whom the data was incidentally collected are in any way a threat to national security or public safety.

When news of this loophole was made public, Senator Ron Wyden (D-Oregon), a member of the Senate Intelligence Committee, stated:

Section 702 [of the FISA Amendments Act] was intended to give the government new authorities to collect the communications of individuals believed to be foreigners outside the US, but the intelligence community has been unable to tell Congress how many Americans have had their communications swept up in that collection. Once Americans' communications are collected, a gap in the law that I call the "back-door searches loophole" allows the government to potentially go through these communications and conduct warrantless searches for the phone calls or emails of law-abiding Americans.

Senator Dianne Feinstein (D-California), chair of the Senate Intelligence Committee, rushed to reassure people that this was not the case—that checks were in place to ensure that the NSA could not search and retain the communications data of American citizens, as did several other members of the Senate Intelligence Committee and President Barack Obama. However, Senator Wyden and fellow Intelligence Committee member Senator Mark Udall (D-Colorado) were not convinced. Both Udall and Wyden did not oppose surveillance—they simply felt that the way Section 702 was written, it did not protect the privacy rights of American citizens. Wyden told the *Guardian* in 2013, "I believe that Congress should reform Section 702 to provide better protections for Americans' privacy, and that this could be done without losing the value that this collection provides." It should be noted that as of the time of this writing, there has been no reform to Section 702 or the FISA Amendments Act in general. The act was to expire on December 31, 2017.

So what is the danger in monitoring the communications of people whose data are inadvertently gathered as part of incidental collection? Those who support government surveillance argue that if you're not doing anything wrong, you don't have anything to worry about. Who cares if the government sees what you're doing, when you're not doing anything wrong?

Surveillance Gone Wrong

The case of Brandon Mayfield shows how innocent people can get caught up in an investigation. In March 2004, terrorists inspired by al-Qaeda bombed the commuter train system in Madrid, Spain, killing 192 people and leaving an estimated 1,800 wounded. When the FBI ran two latent fingerprints that had been recovered from the attack, they found twenty possible matches in their system. One possible match was Mayfield, an attorney from Portland, Oregon. He had been a US Army platoon leader, so his fingerprints were automatically in the FBI's system.

Mayfield's prints were not an exact match, but the FBI looked into his background anyway, and it learned he had converted to Islam when he married his Egyptian wife and that he worshipped at the same mosque in Portland as a group of seven al-Qaeda militants. It also learned that he had represented one of the militants in a child custody case. And so, the FBI requested and obtained a FISA warrant so it could place Mayfield under surveillance—completely ignoring the fact that his fingerprint wasn't a match and there was no concrete reason to suspect he was connected to the Madrid attack.

In its surveillance of Mayfield, the FBI broke into his home and office. It tapped his phone, went through his garbage, surveyed his internet history, and went through documents that were protected by attorney-client privilege. Finding evidence that Mayfield had once taken flight lessons and that someone had done an internet search for Spain on his computer only further convinced the FBI of Mayfield's

The case of lawyer Brandon Mayfield is an example of surveillance gone awry.

guilt, when in reality Mayfield had once taken flight lessons as a hobby, and his daughter was the one who searched for Spain on the internet as part of a school project. Mayfield hadn't traveled internationally for several years and did not have a valid passport, but the FBI was convinced of his guilt. Knowing that the FBI had broken into his home and office, Mayfield was terrified. The FBI ultimately jailed Mayfield for two weeks as a material witness when they couldn't arrest him because they had no evidence of his guilt.

The Spanish National Police repeatedly told the FBI that Mayfield's fingerprints were not a match to the prints found at the attack, but the FBI's surveillance of Mayfield convinced them of his guilt. They only dropped their investigation into Mayfield when the true perpetrator, an Algerian man named Ouhnane Dauod, was arrested. Only then did Mayfield's nightmare at the hands of the FBI end.

That may be true in most cases, but what if a person is doing internet research for some sort of school project on terrorism, for example? Or even just doing research out of idle curiosity? What if someone is interested in learning more about fringe terrorist groups, not because they want to join or support one, but because they're simply curious what motivates these groups? Now imagine that person's data is gathered and surveyed as part of incidental collection. And imagine a terrorist attack happens in the geographical area where that person lives. Suddenly, that person could be the target of an investigation that could complicate his or her life tremendously. As Matthew Harwood, a senior writer/editor for the ACLU, wrote in a 2014 opinion piece for *Al Jazeera America*, the government having access to the data of everyday citizens "can imply guilt where there is none. When investigators have mountains of data on a particular target, it's easy to see only the data points that confirm their theories—especially in counterterrorism investigations when the stakes are so high—while ignoring or downplaying the rest. There doesn't have to be any particular malice on the part of investigators or analysts, although prejudice no doubt comes into play, just circumstantial evidence and the dangerous belief in their intuition."

The Fourth Amendment of the United States Constitution protects citizens' right to privacy, spelling out that "the right of the people to be secure in their persons, houses, papers, and effects, against unreasonable searches and seizures, shall not be violated, and no Warrants shall issue, but upon probable cause, supported by Oath or affirmation, and particularly describing the place to be searched, and the persons or things to be seized." In other words, the government needs probable cause to subject citizens to unreasonable searches. However, that was written long before electronic communications came into play, and thus it has some loopholes that security and intelligence agencies have been able to use over the years to defend their surveillance of citizens.

On one level, the problem with government surveillance is just the violation of a basic human right—the right to privacy. If people want to research something on the internet, in theory they should be able to do so without fear of becoming the subject of an investigation. Perhaps a person is truly just interested in nuclear and chemical reactions, and thus studies bombs and explosives on the internet—in theory, that person may never be a threat to national security or public safety and thus should be free to explore whatever topic he or she wants. But obviously, this becomes a problem when someone studying explosives does so with malicious intent and ultimately a tragedy occurs. And so, there is forever a fine line between respecting people's privacy and preventing incidents that pose a threat to public safety.

On another level, the problem with government surveillance is that it can negatively affect the lives of innocent people, as it did with attorney Brandon Mayfield. It can go beyond a simple invasion of personal privacy and can become a life-changing event for the subject of the surveillance.

The Abuse of Surveillance Systems

Opponents of surveillance also cite the abuse of surveillance systems as a program. In fact, the ACLU details specific ways in which CCTV systems are likely to be misused. First, they point out that surveillance systems can be misused by officials who have access to them. In 1997, for example, a high-ranking police official reportedly used police databases to gather information on people at a gay club and then used that information to blackmail the club attendees who were married and at the club in secret. And a 2016 Associated Press story revealed that across the United States, law enforcement officials use confidential databases for personal purposes, which include gaining personal information about business associates and neighbors, and even stalking people.

The story revealed not just a couple of isolated incidents of this misuse, but rather a fairly significant problem. The AP requested the records of numerous state agencies and police departments in large cities and found nearly six hundred reported incidents of misuse between 2013 and

Voyeurism is one potential problem that comes along with the use of surveillance technology.

2015 that ultimately involved reprimands, counseling, discipline, suspension, or termination for the law enforcement employees. Examples of the cases of misuse included an Ohio police officer who used a law enforcement database to stalk an ex-girlfriend and a Michigan police officer who looked up home addresses of attractive women.

Use of surveillance tools by **voyeurs** is a common problem. In the UK, most of the people who monitor CCTV cameras are male, and studies have found that some operators use the cameras to watch women they find attractive. In one such case, a CCTV operator in Northern Ireland directed a CCTV camera directly into a woman's apartment multiple times over a month-long period, where he was able to watch her walking around her apartment undressed. In another such case, four council workers in Liverpool were accused of the same thing. And in the United States, there have been numerous lawsuits involving surveillance cameras used in private areas, such as restrooms, changing rooms, and locker rooms. Many of these lawsuits involve business owners or employees, but in some cases they involve law enforcement or government officials, such as a 2009 case in West Virginia in which two FBI employees reportedly used surveillance equipment to watch teenage girls try on prom dresses at a charity event.

The ACLU also cites institutional abuse as an issue, where law enforcement and FBI agents have, in the past, used surveillance systems to watch and harass political activists. Given that video surveillance is now often equipped with or used in conjunction with facial-recognition software, it's easy to see how officials could find out an activist's identity by using video footage, and then use that information to further survey or even harass the activist.

The ACLU actually doesn't oppose all surveillance, but it does argue that it's problematic because there is a lack of control over the use of CCTV and other surveillance equipment. Controls exist over the use of audio surveillance, but not over video surveillance, which the ACLU argues is problematic:

> While the Fourth Amendment to the US Constitution offers some protection against video searches conducted by the police, there are currently no general, legally enforceable rules to limit privacy invasions and protect against abuse of CCTV systems. Rules are needed to establish a clear public understanding of such issues as whether video signals are recorded, under what conditions, and how long are they retained; what the criteria are for access to archived video by other government agencies, or by the public; how the rules would be verified and enforced; and what punishments would apply to violators.

The Misuse of Personal Information

Another problem with mass surveillance is the potential for the misuse of personal information. The government isn't the only entity using surveillance techniques—businesses and other companies collect data and personal information, too. Unlike the government, they're not interested in whether you're a potential threat to national security or public safety; they're more interested in things like your buying habits and your likes and interests.

On a simple level, giants Facebook and Amazon provide a good example of this. Based on your Facebook posts and your other activity on the site (for example, posts you like and/or comment on), Facebook recognizes certain patterns and then can target posts to you. If you have liked a bunch of Facebook pages on pugs, for example, you might notice you suddenly start seeing sponsored posts from companies marketing or promoting dog-related items or services.

Similarly, Amazon collects information about you based on your purchases and then uses that information to suggest other products you might like. If you ordered a Jane Austen novel, for example, Amazon will likely suggest other Jane Austen books and other books from Austen's contemporaries that you might like. It might also suggest Jane Austen–related merchandise for you to buy.

Identity theft is a growing problem, particularly as internet retailers gather and store personal information.

Although this data gathering and suggestion making can be slightly annoying (they're not always right on—just because you bought *Pride and Prejudice* doesn't necessarily mean you want a Mr. Darcy tea set, for example), in general it's harmless. But it can become a headache when companies sell your information to other companies, and it can become a very large headache when companies that have your information experience a data breach, and suddenly personal information such as your credit card number, address, and social security number is stolen by a hacker group.

Retail giant Target experienced a data breach in late 2013, when hackers used a third-party vendor of Target's—a refrigeration company—as a way to break into Target's internal network. (They hacked into the refrigeration company's system and determined the company's login to Target's system, and then used that login to breach Target's massive system.) From there, the hackers were able to gain access to the credit and debit card numbers, as well as encrypted PINs, of an estimated forty million people who had shopped at Target and used their cards.

This security breach ended up costing Target $39 million in a settlement with US banks that had been forced to reimburse customers whose card numbers were fraudulently used as a result of the Target hacking. And naturally, it was a massive headache for those consumers.

Similar data breaches have occurred in the health-care industry, too—in fact, such breaches reportedly cost the health-care industry approximately $5.6 billion per year. According to the Office of Civil Rights under the Department of Health and Human Services, in 2015 more than 113 million medical records were compromised. Anthem, a large health insurance provider in the United States, had

78.8 million of its customer records hacked in 2015. And Beth Israel Deaconess Medical Center CIO John Halamka said in 2016 that his hospital faces a hacking attempt every seven seconds.

Why is the health-care industry such a target? Simply put, health records are goldmine. If a credit card number is stolen, that card can quickly be shut down. But that's not the case with health-care records, which contain all the information a hacker needs to steal someone's identity: social security numbers, addresses, names of family members, job information, and so on. Credit agency Experian has said that to hackers, health-care records are worth ten times more than credit card numbers for this very reason.

Sometimes the insurance company or the hospital is the entry point for a hacker, but sometimes, unwittingly, it's the actual patient. Many health-care facilities and insurance companies now have smartphone apps that allow patients to access their health records. The problem is, many of these same apps also allow hackers to access health records because the apps lack appropriate security controls.

The Effectiveness of Surveillance

There are questions, too, about the effectiveness of surveillance—specifically, the effectiveness of video surveillance.

One problem is that for video surveillance to be effective, the people monitoring the video feeds need to be effectively doing their job. Experts on security technology for the US government have found that the attention of people monitoring video feeds tends to drop to below an acceptable level of attention after only twenty minutes of watching.

Another issue is that for really major crimes, such as terrorist attacks, video surveillance is not a particularly effective deterrent. Often, the opposite is true. Some terrorist groups, such as al-Qaeda and ISIS, actually like to take credit for attacks and aren't trying to hide anything. Often they're using suicide bombers to carry out such attacks, and those people have no reason to care whether they're identified via video surveillance—they'll be dead soon anyway. And even for those who don't plan a suicide attack, when it's a terrorist incident, the terrorists are often keen on the attention they get from television coverage, so they don't particularly care if they're identified.

It is thought that video surveillance may help prevent lesser crimes, such as pickpocketing, but even that doesn't seem to be the case. The city of Lincoln, Nebraska, attempted to use surveillance cameras to cut down on crime in the city's downtown district, and the chief of police reported in 2015 that the cameras had not helped the city identify any new suspects or build their case against current ones. The

London's Trafalgar Square attracts tourists and pickpockets. Police use CCTV to try to stop the latter.

number of assaults in the area remained steady, with the average results over a five-year period showing approximately 128 assaults in a year.

According to the ACLU, law enforcement in San Francisco, Los Angeles, Baltimore, Chicago, and Washington, DC, performed similar studies as the chief of police in Lincoln did, and most found similar results—no significant change in crime when surveillance cameras were used. Baltimore was the only city that reported a drop in crime with the use of surveillance cameras.

One reason why video surveillance may be proving largely ineffective in deterring crime in city areas is the displacement effect. The displacement effect describes the fact that criminal activity simply moves outside of the range of the cameras. If cameras are heavily concentrated in the city center, the criminal activity there simply moves outward, where there are fewer cameras. Another theory is that the cameras create a false sense of security among citizens, who then drop their guard and may be more susceptible to criminal acts.

Has Surveillance Gone Too Far?

Many people agree that some level of government surveillance is a reasonable method for trying to ensure public safety and prevent terrorist attacks. However, the question is whether surveillance has gone too far. Have we reached a point where surveillance techniques have taken away people's right to privacy?

Certainly, we don't exist quite in the era Orwell described in *Nineteen Eighty-Four*. We don't walk down hallways filled with monitors showing Big Brother touting the virtues of Newspeak and common thought. We don't have our thoughts monitored by the party, and we aren't essentially brainwashed for having our own opinions.

But we do live in an era in which the government can gain access to our personal communications through incidental collection. We live in an era in which the government can use that data to profile us. We live in an era in which our identities can be stolen or our finances compromised because businesses and corporations are allowed to collect and store our personal data. We live in an era in which law enforcement personnel can, in theory, misuse our personal information for their own gain. And we apparently live in an era when the CIA and allied agencies can use software tools that can, according to the *New York Times*, "break into smartphones, computers and even Internet-connected televisions." The *Times* story, based on documents released by WikiLeaks, says the CIA and related agencies can bypass encryption on cell phone and messaging services.

The story also stated that cybersecurity experts believe the ability of internet-connected televisions to record and transmit conversations is a potentially dangerous vulnerability that can be exploited by hackers.

Has it gone too far? Does it outweigh the benefit that comes from having the government able to monitor potential criminal activity to prevent terrorist attacks and solve crimes?

Certainly, there's a fine line that is difficult to define. At some point, the systems designed to protect people can be seen as putting them at risk. The question is: Where does that point lie?

News of the DNC email leaks dominated the Democratic National Convention in 2016.

CHAPTER 4

Current Surveillance and Looking Ahead

A s we've moved into the later part of the 2010s, government surveillance is particularly in the news. The news of the NSA's PRISM system broke in 2013 and brought with it an outcry over the invasion of people's privacy, and then shortly thereafter came reports of China hacking into United States servers and systems. And, of course, with the 2016 election came reports of Russia hacking into systems in the United States, specifically the servers of the Democratic National Committee.

Surveillance started centuries—even millennia—ago with people spying on others and sharing confidential information, as well as intercepting written communications. It evolved into **wiretapping** telephones and telegraphs, then into video surveillance. And finally, as the internet has become ubiquitous and technology has increased in sophistication, we have entered an era of electronic surveillance of internet communications, data, and usage. We're not yet into an era of monitoring people's thoughts, like Orwell described in *Nineteen Eighty-Four*, but in some ways we're not that far off.

So the question is: What do today's surveillance threats mean? And what's being done to protect citizens' privacy?

Hacking in the Name of Competition

In May 2014, federal prosecutors handed down a thirty-one-count indictment charging members of the **People's Liberation Army** (PLA) of China with cyber theft and other related crimes. The hackers' motive? Undercutting US competition in numerous industries. China and the United States have long jockeyed for top positions in the global marketplace, and by hacking into US servers, the Chinese could gain access to trade secrets that could weaken the United States' position in that marketplace.

According to the prosecutors, the PLA hackers stole specifications for high-tech nuclear power plants, stole manufacturing plans for solar panels, hacked into US Steel computers that controlled access to US Steel buildings, stole network credentials for employees at Alleghany Technologies Incorporated (a steelmaker), and surveyed emails at Alcoa (an aluminum manufacturer) and the United Steelworkers union.

The goal of the hackers, the prosecutors believe, was to capitalize on all the research and development the United States had spent years (and untold amounts of money) doing. Chinese steel was not up to the standards of US steel in terms of being high in quality and low in weight, and if hackers could gain access to the US findings for how to manufacture high-quality, lightweight steel, they could save themselves money and time in research and development. Their motives were similar for hacking into companies working on nuclear power and solar power.

In 2015, China was believed to be behind a data hacking scandal that resulted in the personal data of millions of current, former, and prospective federal employees being compromised. (The hack was originally thought to affect

Hackers come from everywhere and can be difficult to pinpoint. They are very good at hiding their tracks.

approximately four million records, but later estimates put the number of people affected somewhere between eighteen million and twenty-one million.) The Chinese government denied the allegations, but US officials believe Chinese hackers were indeed the source and that their motive was to gain more information about US systems that the Chinese can use in future cyberattacks.

In 2016, the House of Representatives' Science, Space, and Technology Committee released an investigative report detailing that Chinese spies had hacked into computers at the **Federal Deposit Insurance Corporation** (FDIC) over a three-year period from 2010 to 2013, and that FDIC officials had tried to cover up the security breach. The FDIC holds incredibly sensitive personal information about millions of Americans, thanks to its access to the records of 4,500 banks and savings institutions.

Hacking by the Chinese actually decreased in 2016, thanks to an anti-hacking agreement the Chinese signed with the Obama administration in September 2015. In the agreement, both governments agreed that neither would "conduct or knowingly support cyber-enabled theft of intellectual property, including trade secrets or other confidential business information, with the intent of providing competitive advantages to companies or commercial sectors." The founder of CrowdStrike, a cybersecurity firm, reported a 90 percent decrease in commercial hacking of US firms by hackers acting on behalf of the Chinese government. United States intelligence agencies also confirmed a significant drop in commercial hacking by Chinese sources.

This agreement hasn't caused a drop in hacking to steal national security information, but it was not expected to—the NSA hacks into Chinese servers to spy on their national security secrets as well, so it's expected that the Chinese government will do the same. The agreement was intended to curb hacking for commercial gain, and so far it has served its purpose. Whether that trend will continue remains to be seen.

Russian Hacking Disrupts a Presidential Election

Hacking by Russians into US servers created a huge threat to US security in 2016. The suspected goal of the Russian

Rumors of Russian hacking to influence the outcome of the 2016 election plagued President Donald Trump.

hackers? To disrupt the 2016 elections, particularly the one for president.

Some of the details on the Russian attacks are hazy. At the time of this writing, it's unknown whether the Russian government wanted to ensure that Donald Trump was elected president, or whether it simply wanted to cause chaos in the election as a sort of "warning shot" to show what it is capable of.

Admiral Michael S. Rogers, director of the NSA and head of the United States Cyber Command, felt it was more than a warning shot, saying:

There shouldn't be any doubt in anybody's mind. This was not something that was done casually, this was not something that was done by chance, this was not a target that was selected purely arbitrarily. This was a conscious effort by a nation-state to attempt to achieve a specific effect.

It's also unknown exactly how much the Russians accomplished with their hacking. Did they simply obtain and leak enough damaging material about Democrat Hillary Clinton that Donald Trump won the election fair and square? Or did their hacking physically alter the election results? As of this writing, no evidence of the latter had emerged.

What is known is that the Russians did indeed hack into US servers and obtain access to confidential information, which was then leaked to the public on WikiLeaks and via other sources. Some of these leaks were of personal emails, which were very embarrassing to those who wrote them. And while it's suspected that they hacked into both Republican National Committee and Democratic National Committee servers, it's clear that they focused heavily on DNC servers. Debbie Wasserman Schultz resigned from her job as the chairman of the DNC after the emails were leaked.

Russia, under the leadership of President Vladimir Putin, was keen to see Trump win the election, and up until the very end of the election, Trump was the underdog—early polls showed that Clinton would easily win the presidency. Still, Russia hoped that Trump would emerge the victor, and at the very least, it released enough damaging information about Clinton and the Democratic campaign to help bolster Trump's chances of winning. (Whether Trump had anything to do with this Russian interference is currently unknown. Trump claims he did not.)

Trump was largely thought to be the presidential candidate more "friendly" to Russia's interests, and thus Putin and the Russian government endorsed him as president. However, the United States election process is confined to United States citizens, and thus Russia should have absolutely no say in it. Even so, it attempted to influence the election in a subversive manner. The job was done by two separate groups of Russian hackers, nicknamed Cozy Bear and Fancy Bear. Cozy Bear is thought to be associated with the FSB—Russia's main security agency—while Fancy Bear is thought to be associated with the GRU, Russia's military intelligence agency.

It is thought that Cozy Bear and Fancy Bear worked independently, but both on behalf of Russian agencies—and both infiltrating the DNC. Ultimately, thousands of hacked emails and documents were released, first on a website called DC Leaks, and then later on WikiLeaks, the widely known nonprofit that publishes classified information and news leaks from anonymous sources. Strategically, WikiLeaks published several thousand emails a day, rather than publishing them all at once, as it was thought that a sustained, systematic attack on Clinton's character and her campaign would be more damaging than one massive attack. News outlets picked up on the information published by WikiLeaks, and the negative news spread. (WikiLeaks founder Julian Assange has publicly stated his distaste for Clinton.)

Did the strategy work? It's impossible to know for sure. Trump did indeed win the election, but whether he won because Russian hackers obtained private information and then systematically published it in the most effectively damaging manner possible, or whether he won fair and square because the voters preferred him as the future president, cannot be determined. The one thing that can be stated as fact is that the Russian hacking and subsequent publication of damaging information didn't help Clinton's campaign.

How Can Citizens Be Protected?

The Russian hacking of the 2016 presidential campaign is troubling on a number of levels. Hillary Clinton lost several crucial states by small margins. If any of these states were lost due to Russian interference, it's deeply troubling that the American election could have been influenced by the actions of an outside country.

On a more personal level, consider the implications of the hacking: Thousands of private emails were made public, and an organization as large as the DNC was unable to prevent it. How could the average person, with access only to standard virus-scan software and firewalls, protect himself or herself. It's clear that if someone wanted to, he or she could easily access the email of *any* person. It's not particularly likely to happen to the average person, simply because the average person's emails aren't of that much interest to the general public. But it *could* happen, and that is a troubling thought.

And on a larger scale, how can citizens be protected from potential terrorists while at the same time maintaining their own right to privacy?

The PATRIOT Act

In reaction to the terrorist attacks of September 11, 2001, Congress and President George W. Bush passed the USA PATRIOT Act, which contained provisions that would allow the US government to intercept and obstruct suspected terrorists. Some of the measures allowed by the act included the use of roving wiretaps, business records searches, and surveillance of individuals suspected of terrorist ties or interests but who were not officially affiliated with any terrorist group.

Portions of the PATRIOT Act expired in 2015 but were replaced by the USA FREEDOM Act, which was passed on June 2, 2015. However, there is one big difference between the FREEDOM Act and the PATRIOT Act. The PATRIOT Act allowed for mass collection of communications data by the NSA and related agencies, whereas the FREEDOM Act put strong limitations on that practice. It was a change that earned praise from the ACLU, which called it "a milestone," and from senators such as Patrick Leahy (D-Vermont), who worked to pass the FREEDOM Act for two years and declared, "It is time to do our jobs for the American people— to protect their privacy and maintain our national security."

Whistleblowers and WikiLeaks

Some would say that one way Americans have been able to protect their right to privacy is thanks to whistleblowers like Edward Snowden and organizations such as WikiLeaks. Others would argue that whistleblowers may cause an invasion of privacy in the same way that organizations like the NSA do.

Whistleblowing is nothing new—Benjamin Franklin became one of the first American whistleblowers when he shared confidential letters proving that the governor of Massachusetts had knowingly misled Parliament due to his interest in building up the military in North America. Military

Whistleblower Edward Snowden exposed the surveillance tactics of the NSA.

analyst Daniel Ellsberg leaked a classified document detailing military decision making in Vietnam from the end of World War II to 1968. The document, known as the Pentagon Papers, was given to a reporter from the *New York Times* in 1971. It fanned the flames of opposition to the already unpopular Vietnam War. And perhaps most famously, the anonymous Deep Throat (decades later revealed to be the former associate director of the FBI) gave *Washington Post* reporters Bob

Woodward and Carl Bernstein information that helped them detail White House involvement in the Watergate break-in, which ultimately led to President Richard Nixon's resignation amid scandal and an impending impeachment.

Whistleblowing has been going on for centuries and has been increasingly prominent in recent decades, leading up to revelations by Edward Snowden, a former federal contractor who exposed information about the NSA's surveillance of United States citizens. Snowden leaked thousands of confidential documents regarding NSA surveillance to the *Guardian* (a British news outlet), the *Washington Post*, the *New York Times*, and several other global media sources.

The response to these leaks has been mixed. Some feel Snowden is a traitor who should be prosecuted for his acts. The United States Department of Justice, for example, has charged Snowden with theft of government property and with violating the Espionage Act of 1917. Others consider Snowden a hero and say that without Snowden's efforts, the NSA would still be conducting surveillance on American citizens without cause or justification.

Whistleblowers like Edward Snowden need organizations designed to spread information that may otherwise stay hidden. Such is the case with WikiLeaks, the nonprofit internet publishing outlet founded by Julian Assange. And, just as public opinion on Snowden's actions is mixed, so are opinions on WikiLeaks' actions.

WikiLeaks has published countless documents and classified information from numerous sources on various topics, ranging from classified information on wars in the Middle East to confidential documents and emails from the DNC regarding the 2016 election. At times, the organization has been hailed as heroic for its role in exposing government

Julian Assange, the founder of WikiLeaks, has sought asylum to avoid prosecution in the United States.

cover-ups and corruption. At other times, however, WikiLeaks has been every bit as careless as the NSA in violating the public's right to privacy. For example, in 2016 WikiLeaks published three hundred thousand of Turkish prime minister Recep Erdogan's emails. In doing so, the site exposed a spreadsheet of nearly every female voter in Turkey, including home addresses and cell phone numbers, as well as sensitive personal information for numerous members of Turkey's ruling political party. And similarly, when WikiLeaks posted the DNC emails, it also exposed personal information of DNC donors, including social security numbers and credit card numbers.

In a 2015 opinion piece written for the *Boston Globe*, Michael A. Cohen described how it took him—a writer, not a hacker—a mere twenty minutes on WikiLeaks to obtain "a credit card number, medical information, private email addresses, salary data, and plenty else that most people wouldn't want available on a searchable database." Cohen went on to say, "This kind of cyberattack is a greater threat to people's privacy than anything revealed in the Snowden/NSA leaks, which became a **cause célèbre** for some of the same people chortling over the Sony leaks [in which WikiLeaks posted data stolen from Sony Pictures]."

So are organizations like WikiLeaks a help in protecting citizens' right to privacy, or are they a hindrance? The answer depends on who you ask, although certainly there is enough evidence to support either side of the argument.

Surveillance: Positive or Negative?

Clearly, there are compelling points on both sides of this argument. Government surveillance can be a way to ensure

Microsoft legal officer Brad Smith has called for cyber protection of civilians during peacetime.

public safety and national security, and in an era when terrorism is a real threat, it can be comforting to know that organizations exist to keep an eye on potential threats to our nation.

But at the same time, the lines are blurry as to where surveillance stops and intrusion into people's privacy begins. Incidental collection of data and blanket surveillance compromise people's privacy, as do the actions of external hackers.

The problem is so worrisome that Microsoft legal officer Brad Smith called for a digital Geneva Convention to protect civilians from cybercrimes.

During a speech given in February 2017 at the RSA cybersecurity conference San Francisco, Smith said:

> Just as the Fourth Geneva Convention has long protected civilians in times of war, we now need a Digital Geneva Convention that will commit governments to protecting civilians from nation-state attacks in times of peace. And just as the Fourth Geneva Convention recognized that the protection of civilians required the active involvement of the Red Cross, protection against nation-state cyberattacks requires the active assistance of technology companies.

As we continue in a technologically progressive era, no doubt citizens will continue to struggle with the question of whether surveillance is a protection or an invasion.

December 15, 1791 The Fourth Amendment to the Constitution, written in the Bill of Rights, is adopted. It establishes protection for the privacy of US citizens, saying that citizens may not be subject to "unreasonable searches and seizures."

1890 With the invention of the telephone, wiretapping becomes possible.

June 4, 1928 Supreme Court approves wiretapping in *Olmstead v. United States*.

August 1945 Project Shamrock begins. It allows the Armed Forces Security Agency and its successor, the NSA, to read all telegraphic data entering or exiting the United States. The data came from companies such as Western Union and RCA.

November 4, 1952 NSA is formed under the order of President Harry Truman.

December 18, 1967 In *Katz v. United States*, the Supreme Court overturns wiretapping or listening to a citizen's phone conversations, even on a public payphone, without probable cause.

June 19, 1968 Omnibus Crime Control and Safe Streets Act restricts wiretapping in general but protects the president's authorization to use surveillance tools in matters of national security.

June 17, 1972 Under the order of President Richard Nixon, the Committee to Re-elect the President attempts to wiretap the DNC headquarters. The ensuing scandal, called Watergate, eventually leads to Nixon's resignation.

May 1975 Project Shamrock is shut down.

October 25, 1978 FISA signed into law by President Jimmy Carter.

October 26, 1986 Electronic Communications Privacy Act is signed into law by President Ronald Reagan. The act makes it harder for the government to obtain search warrants for electronic communications.

October 26, 2001 USA PATRIOT Act signed into law by President George W. Bush.

December 16, 2005 *New York Times* story exposes the fact that the NSA had wiretapped thousands of United States citizens without warrants.

2007 NSA's PRISM begins collecting data from United States providers.

July 10, 2008 FISA Amendments Act signed into law by President Bush.

June 2013 Edward Snowden releases NSA documents proving surveillance of US citizens.

2016 Russian hackers infiltrate the DNC system, potentially affecting the outcome of the 2016 US presidential election.

ACLU An acronym for the American Civil Liberties Union, an organization that works to preserve the civil rights and liberties of the American people.

antithesis Someone or something that is a direct opposite of another person or object.

black chamber A government office or department at which communications are monitored and, if necessary, decoded.

cause célèbre A controversial issue that attracts public attention.

corporal punishment Physical punishment, such as spanking.

cryptographer A person who writes or breaks codes.

czarist Describes the rule of Russia when it was under an emperor (prior to 1917).

dashcam A video camera mounted on a vehicle's dashboard.

entrapment Tricking someone into committing a crime so they can then be prosecuted and/or punished.

fascist A rigidly authoritarian person who favors the nation above the person, often is racist, and supports the suppression of opposing views.

Federal Deposit Insurance Corporation The government entity that insures most private bank deposits against bank failure.

Geneva Conventions Four treaties and three protocols among nations governing the treatment of people, prisoners of war, and wounded soldiers during wartime.

heretic A person holding dissenting beliefs from an established religion.

indict To formally charge or accuse of a crime.

Iron Curtain An imagined barrier separating the Eastern and Western Blocs in Europe after World War II and before the fall of the Soviet Union.

ISIL Stands for Islamic State of Iraq and the Levant, an Islamic extremist group that wants to establish a caliphate run according to sharia law. The group is also known as ISIS, or Islamic State of Iraq and Syria.

jihad The struggle or fight against opponents of Islam.

martyrdom To die or be killed for a religion or for holding religious beliefs.

People's Liberation Army The unified organization of the land, sea, and air forces of China's military.

perjury Telling a lie after taking an oath in court.

Reign of Terror A period of violence from September 5, 1793, to July 27, 1794, during the French Revolution. There were seventeen thousand people officially executed and an estimated ten thousand others who died in prison.

Stasi The state security organization of the German Democratic Republic (East Germany), abolished after the reunification of East and West Germany.

Taliban A fundamentalist militia in Afghanistan under the umbrella of Islam. It is generally considered to be an extremist movement.

totalitarianism A centralized, dictatorial government structure.

treasonous Something that betrays one's country.

voyeur A person who gets pleasure from watching other people, usually by looking into their homes.

whistleblower A person who informs on an organization that is involved in illegal activities or displays questionable ethics.

wiretapping Placing a listening device on a telephone line in order to hear phone conversations.

Books

Brock, George. *The Right to Be Forgotten: Privacy and the Media in the Digital Age*. London, UK: I. B. Tauris, 2016.

Cropf, Robert A., and Timothy C. Bagwell. *Ethical Issues and Citizen Rights in the Era of Digital Government Surveillance*. Hershey, PA: IGI Global, 2016.

Greenwald, Glenn. *No Place to Hide: Edward Snowden, the NSA, and the US Surveillance State*. New York: Metropolitan Books, 2014.

Harding, Luke. *The Snowden Files: The Inside Story of the World's Most Wanted Man*. New York: Vintage Books, 2014.

WikiLeaks and Julian Assange. *The WikiLeaks Files: The World According to US Empire*. London, UK: Verso, 2016.

Video

Government Surveillance: This Is Just the Beginning.

https://www.ted.com/talks/christopher_soghoian_
government_surveillance_this_is_just_the_beginning

This TED Talk from 2013 by privacy researcher Christopher Soghoian describes the tools governments are purchasing to spy on their own citizens and how this problem will increase.

Julian Assange: A Modern Day Hero?
Inside the World of WikiLeaks

This 2012 documentary available on DVD investigates the founder of WikiLeaks and his organization.

Organizations

ACLU

https://www.aclu.org

The official site of the American Civil Liberties Union, an excellent resource about citizens' right to privacy.

National Security Agency

https://www.nsa.gov

The official NSA website contains news and information about what the NSA does.

WikiLeaks

https://www.wikileaks.org_

The biggest online publisher of material provided by whistleblowers.

Books

Carrier, Jerry. *Hard Right Turn: Assassination of the American Left—A History.* New York: Algora Publishing, 2015.

Farago, Ladislas. *Burn After Reading: The Espionage History of World War II.* Annapolis, MD: Naval Institute Press, 2012.

Murphy, Cullen. *God's Jury: The Inquisition and the Making of the Modern World.* New York: Houghton Mifflin Harcourt, 2012.

Sarwar, Cal. *The Cell, the Wolf, and the Faith: They Love Death More Than We Love Life.* Pennsauken, NJ: BookBaby: 2014.

Slaveski, Filip. *The Soviet Occupation of Germany: Hunger, Mass Violence and the Struggle for Peace, 1945–1947.* Cambridge, UK: Cambridge University Press, 2013.

Stedall, Robert. *The Survival of the Crown, Volume II: The Return to Authority of the Scottish Crown Following Mary Queen of Scots' Deposition From the Throne, 1567–1603.* East Sussex, UK: Book Guild Ltd., 2014.

Sun Tzu. *The Art of War.* Hollywood, FL: Simon & Brown, 2016.

Online Articles

Akpan, Nsikan. "Has Health Care Hacking Become an Epidemic?" PBS NewsHour, March 23, 2016. http://www.pbs.org/newshour/updates/has-health-care-hacking-become-an-epidemic.

Baker, Al, and Marc Santora. "San Bernardino Attackers Discussed Jihad in Private Messages, F.B.I. Says." *New York Times*, December 16, 2015. http://www.nytimes.com/2015/12/17/us/san-bernardino-attackers-discussed-jihad-in-private-messages-fbi-says.html.

Ball, James, and Spencer Ackerman. "NSA Loophole Allows Warrantless Search for US Citizens' Emails and Phone Calls." *Guardian*, August 9, 2013. https://www.theguardian.com/world/2013/aug/09/nsa-loophole-warrantless-searches-email-calls.

Bracy, Jedidiah. "Ethics and the Privacy Harms of WikiLeaks." International Association of Privacy Professionals, July 26, 2016. https://iapp.org/news/a/ethics-and-the-privacy-harms-of-wikileaks.

Bryant, Ben. "GCHQ Can Access Raw Data from NSA Without a Warrant, Secret Policies Disclose." Vice News, October 29, 2014. https://news.vice.com/

article/gchq-can-access-raw-data-from-nsa-without-a-warrant-secret-policies-disclose.

Brzezinski, Mika. "Commentary on Surveillance, Censorship, and Elements of Modern Day Inquisition." MSNBC, January 27, 2012. https://preview-archives. nbclearn.com/portal/site/k-12/flatview?cuecard=56690.

Cantor, David, Bonnie Fisher, Susan Chibnall, Reanna Townsend, et. al. "Report on the AAU Campus Climate Survey on Sexual Assault and Sexual Misconduct." Association of American Universities (AAU), September 21, 2015. https://www.aau.edu/ uploadedFiles/AAU_Publications/AAU_Reports/ Sexual_Assault_Campus_Survey/AAU_Campus_ Climate_Survey_12_14_15.pdf.

"Civilian Agency Records RG 216." National Archives. Accessed March 3, 2017. https://www.archives.gov/ research/holocaust/finding-aid/civilian/rg-216.html.

Cohen, Jon. "Most Americans Back NSA Tracking Phone Records, Prioritize Probes Over Privacy." *Washington Post*, June 10, 2013. https://www.washingtonpost. com/politics/most-americans-support-nsa-tracking-phone-records-prioritize-investigations-over-privacy/2013/06/10/51e721d6-d204-11e2-9f1a-1a7cdee20287_story.html?utm_term=.d7078359143e.

Cohen, Michael A. "Where's the Wikileaks Outrage?" *Boston Globe*, April 24, 2015. https://www. bostonglobe.com/opinion/editorials/2015/04/24/ wikileaks-and-media-shrinking-our-zone-privacy/6emuRl1zP4Iyl2frKo46uK/story.html.

Dilanian, Ken. "Russia May Be Hacking Us More, but China Is Hacking Us Much Less." NBC News, October 12, 2016. http://www.nbcnews.com/news/us-news/ russia-may-be-hacking-us-more-china-hacking-us-much-n664836.

Editors of Encyclopedia Britannica. "Reign of Terror." Encyclopedia Britannica, updated May 15, 2015. https://www.britannica.com/event/Reign-of-Terror.

Farris, June Pachuta. "The Red Pencil: Censorship in Russia and the Soviet Union." University of Chicago Library News, May 9, 2013. http://news.lib.uchicago. edu/blog/2013/05/09/the-red-pencil-censorship-in-russia-the-soviet-union.

Gellman, Barton, and Laura Poitras. "U.S., British Intelligence Mining Data From Nine U.S. Internet Companies in Broad Secret Program." *Washington*

Post, June 7, 2013. https://www.washingtonpost.
com/investigations/us-intelligence-mining-data-
from-nine-us-internet-companies-in-broad-secret-
program/2013/06/06/3a0c0da8-cebf-11e2-8845-
d970ccb04497_story.html?utm_term=.8b2ec8af9ab2.

Harwood, Matthew. "The Terrifying Surveillance Case
of Brandon Mayfield." *Al Jazeera America*, February 8,
2014. http://america.aljazeera.com/opinions/2014/2/
the-terrifying-surveillancecaseofbrandonmayfield.html.

Howerton, Jason. "Here Is the Pro-NSA Surveillance
Argument." *Blaze*, June 10, 2013. http://www.
theblaze.com/stories/2013/06/10/here-is-the-pro-nsa-
surveillance-argument.

"Impairing Education: Corporal Punishment of Students
with Disabilities in US Public Schools." American Civil
Liberties Union, August 2009. https://www.aclu.org/sites/
default/files/pdfs/humanrights/impairingeducation.pdf.

"The Inquisition: Alive and Well After 800 Years." *All
Things Considered*, NPR, January 14, 2012. http://www.
npr.org/2012/01/15/144907141/the-inquisition-alive-
and-well-after-800-years.

Kelly, Erin. "Senate Approves USA Freedom Act." *USA Today*, June 2, 2015. http://www.usatoday.com/story/news/politics/2015/06/02/patriot-act-usa-freedom-act-senate-vote/28345747.

Kelly, Heather. "After Boston: The Pros and Cons of Surveillance Cameras." CNN, April 26, 2013. http://www.cnn.com/2013/04/26/tech/innovation/security-cameras-boston-bombings.

Kutz, Gregory D. "Seclusions and Restraints: Selected Cases of Death and Abuse at Public and Private Schools and Treatment Centers." United States Government Accountability Office, May 19, 2009. http://www.gao.gov/new.items/d09719t.pdf.

Landler, Mark, and Dalia Sussman. "Poll Finds Strong Acceptance for Public Surveillance." *New York Times*, April 30, 2013. http://www.nytimes.com/2013/05/01/us/poll-finds-strong-acceptance-for-public-surveillance.html.

Lierberman, Joseph I., and Susan M. Collins. "A Ticking Time Bomb: Counterterrorism Lessons from the U.S. Government's Failure to Prevent the Fort Hood Attack." US Senate Committee on Homeland Security and Governmental Affairs, February 3, 2011. http://

www.hsgac.senate.gov//imo/media/doc/Fort_Hood/FortHoodReport.pdf?attempt=2.

Lipton, Eric, David E. Sanger, and Scott Shane. "The Perfect Weapon: How Russian Cyberpower Invaded the U.S." *New York Times*, December 13, 2016. http://www.nytimes.com/2016/12/13/us/politics/russia-hack-election-dnc.html.

Orwell, George. "Letter to Noel Willmett." May 18, 1944. http://www.thedailybeast.com/articles/2013/08/12/george-orwell-s-letter-on-why-he-wrote-1984.html.

Pagliery, Jose. "What Were China's Hacker Spies After?" CNN, May 19, 2014. http://money.cnn.com/2014/05/19/technology/security/china-hackers.

"Secret Policy Reveals GCHQ Can Get Warrantless Access to Bulk NSA Data." National Council for Civil Liberties, October 29, 2014. https://www.liberty-human-rights.org.uk/news/press-releases/secret-policy-reveals-gchq-can-get-warrantless-access-bulk-nsa-data.

Shane, Scott, Mark Mazzetti, and Matthew Rosenberg. "WikiLeaks Releases Trove of Alleged C.I.A. Hacking Documents." *New York Times*, March 7, 2017. https://www.nytimes.com/2017/03/07/world/europe/wikileaks-cia-hacking.html?hp&action=click&pgtype=Homepag

e&clickSource=story-heading&module=first-column-region&region=top-news&WT.nav=top-news&_r=0.

Sinozich, Sofi, and Lynn Langton. "Rape and Sexual Assault Victimization Among College-Aged Females, 1995–2013." Department of Justice, Office of Justice Programs, Bureau of Justice Statistics, December 2014. https://www.bjs.gov/content/pub/pdf/rsavcaf9513.pdf.

Stambor, Zak. "How Reliable Is Eyewitness Testimony?" American Psychological Association, April 2006. http://www.apa.org/monitor/apr06/eyewitness.aspx.

Strohm, Chris, and Margaret Talev. "China Vows to Curb Commercial Hacking in Agreement With U.S." Bloomberg Politics, September 25, 2015. https://www.bloomberg.com/politics/articles/2015-09-25/obama-says-u-s-china-agree-to-curb-hacking-for-trade-secrets.

"2016 Data Breach Category Summary." Identity Theft Resource Center, December 13, 2016. http://www.idtheftcenter.org/images/breach/DataBreachReport_2016.pdf.

Welsh, Brandon C., and David P. Farrington. "Public Area CCTV and Crime Prevention: An Updated Systematic Review and Meta-Analysis." *Justice Quarterly*,

October 2009. http://www.tandfonline.com/doi/ abs/10.1080/07418820802506206#preview.

"What's Wrong With Public Video Surveillance?" ACLU. Accessed March 3, 2017. https://www.aclu.org/other/ whats-wrong-public-video-surveillance.

Zurcher, Anthony. "Roman Empire to the NSA: A World History of Government Spying." BBC News, November 1, 2013. http://www.bbc.com/news/magazine-24749166.

Page numbers in **boldface** are illustrations. Entries in **boldface** are glossary terms.

Cathleen Small is an author and editor. She has written more than two dozen books for academic publishers, on topics ranging from technology to war to politics. Cathleen resides in the San Francisco Bay Area with her husband and two young sons.